Planepack

THE ART OF TRAVELLING LIGHT

Planepack

THE ART OF TRAVELLING LIGHT

with Slobodanka Graham

Published by BGPublishers
www.bgpublishers.com.au
© 2019 Bobby Graham Publishers
www.planepack.com.au

All rights reserved

Cover and book design by Elise Knotek, Stripe Design
with illustrations by Slobodanka Graham
Digital editions produced by SunTecIndia
www.suntecindia.com

First edition 2019

The articles in this book first appeared in Planepack 2017-18
www.planepack.com.au

ISBN: 978-0-6486686-2-6 (digital)
ISBN: 978-0-9874041-5-2 (print)

Hello Planepack!

Travel is one of life's pleasures. To discover new lands, cultures and foods, to experience how other people live and work, is enriching and rewarding. I like to travel and enjoy life without the burden of baggage.

Since 2010, I've flown with carry on hand luggage only. That's one hand-held bag, weighing seven kilograms (15.5 pounds) when full.

In this book, I will show you how you too can travel light. Planepack is full of tips and advice and interesting stories for light travellers. ››

Leave the crowds and queues behind as you board planes, buses, trains, boats and cars. With Planepack you'll learn how to exit airports quickly.

Travel light doesn't mean you have to skimp on style. With Planepack, you travel light and dress well at the same time. A curated travel wardrobe is minimal and stylish at the same time.

There are many benefits to light travel. Best of all, with carry on only, your luggage is never delayed or lost by the airline.

At Planepack, you will find many more tips and stories as we provide advice on how to travel light.

Happy light travels!

Slobodanka

Contents

Introduction	9
How to travel the first time with carry on bags only	15
How to be a good light traveller: the Ten Commandments	23
How to overcome your addiction to checked luggage	35
What colour is your wardrobe?	47
What's the Planepack essential packing list?	53
Cosmetics and toiletries: what to pack?	59
My luggage, my father and his ashes (lost luggage story #1)	69

Travel light young

'Are you going to be varm enuff? Haff you taken a jersey? Verr is your handbag? Ai, Bobby - houww can you go out like dat?'

Mimi, my mother, bristled with exasperation: no handbag? What would the world think?

'I'm fine, Mommy! This is 1972 - not 1952!'

I twirled around before heading out the door.
Sixteen years old, with the whole world to explore, I could never be bothered with carrying *things*. Who cared if I got cold? I had love to warm me! Who needs a bag? My house key was folded into a R10 note inside my pocket: I was fine.

Travel light

My mother and I shared a love of fashion. She never taught me to travel lightly. I learnt that all by myself.

I started young.

Exploring our streets, I climbed every wall and every tree, unencumbered by toys or gadgets, dodging grumpy neighbors and befriending dogs. Our street gang of neighborhood children criss-crossed yards and gardens, playing and tumbling through houses and flats. We never wanted *things*; we wanted life.

But what my mother taught me was to leave things behind.

Traveling less light

My mother was one of those mothers who always worried about my well being: Did I have a coat? Was I wearing a vest? So you would have thought she'd advise me to travel lightly, but you'd be wrong.

A long time ago, packing for my first trip to Europe, I squeezed 14 t-shirts into my already bulging suitcase. My mother watched as I struggled:

'Haff you taken warm tings?' she asked.

'Of course, I have Mommy,' I responded, 'and anyway it's going to be warm there.'

When *she* travelled, she took with her as much as she possibly could.

She saw it as a challenge to fly with more than she could carry. My mother would pin jerseys into the sleeves of her coat so that she could wear the jersey *and* the coat in the cabin. She swathed herself in shawls for the trip, claiming she suffered chills.

'Why do you need all of those scarves, Mommy? They give you blankets on the plane, you know?'

'But I vill get cold. My poor knees; I have to put someting over dem. Dose air hostesses never bring me nutting,' she claimed, patting her knees as if to confirm their plight.

Traveling even heavier

Her luggage was always 10 kilos overweight, socks stuffed with bottles of rakija; presents from her Serbian family.

She willed herself through customs and was never pulled over for excess baggage or alcohol. But she handicapped herself, lugging bags, shopping baskets, suitcases, and trailing fabrics, from plane to plane.

When I travelled with her - only once did we make that trip to Europe together - I thought I'd die. We negotiated the airports with my pushing her wheelchair, balancing her walking stick and heaving her bags through customs. I never recovered from that struggle. It was the moment that defined Planepack.

Planepack:
the art of traveling light

Planepack is my personal philosophy of flying and traveling light. I no longer lug bags in and out of planes, boats and trains. I don't go near baggage claim. And my luggage is never lost. Planepack frees me to travel lightly and nimbly. How do I do that? I fly and travel with carry on hand luggage only.

In Planepack, I write about travel, the art of packing light, and how to do that with minimum fuss and maximum pleasure.

How to travel the first time with carry on bags only

'HOW DO YOU DO IT, BOBBY? YOU FLY WITH HAND LUGGAGE ONLY? YOU HAVE TO TEACH ME TO PACK AND TRAVEL LIKE YOU DO!' I'VE RECEIVED THIS QUESTION - AND THE RESPONSE - A LOT, WHICH IS WHY I STARTED PLANEPACK, A WEBSITE THAT PROVIDES TIPS, ADVICE AND STORIES FOR LIGHT TRAVELLERS.

Since 2010, I've travelled with carry on luggage only. Europe, Africa, Asia, Australia, New Zealand - it doesn't matter where I go, I no longer lug suitcases. I pack and carry 7 kgs only - and you can do it too.

If you want to know how to pack and travel lightly, this is it: Planepack is my light travel philosophy. It's my tao of travel: how I pack, fly and travel with carry on luggage only.

Planepack *travel light principle*
#1

Plan your light luggage

My first Planepack travel light principle is to plan and prepare:

- ↪ *where* am I going
- ↪ how *long* will I stay
- ↪ what *must* I take with me
- ↪ what will I *do* while away

Once I've covered those off, it's easy to pack accordingly. Next step: I use the *lightest* possible carry on luggage. Mine is a roll-on spinner suitcase. You might prefer a backpack. Whichever you choose, do so carefully: your carry on bag is your best travel friend.

Planepack travel light principle #2

Pack your light luggage

My second Planepack travel light principle is to pack with consideration:

Packing light is an art: roll, fold, vacuum pack - you choose the style that suits you best. But your *contents* determine how light or how heavy your bag is. I weigh, weigh and weigh again to get in under the average 7 kgs limit. I research airlines' websites for their particular weight restrictions before flying with them.

Planepack travel light principle
#3

Carry on light luggage

My third Planepack travel light principle is not to burden myself with unnecessary stuff.

For the past few trips, I've cut back on things I take with me: no unnecessary clothes; fewer appliances; no knick-knacks - just the essentials. But I carry the 'killer' necklace for an evening out. My packing might be plain, but I still like a little glamour.

Planepack travel light principle

#4

Enjoy the trip with light luggage only

My most valuable Planepack principle is to enjoy the trip.
No lifting heavy bags in and out of cars; up stairs; into
minute lifts; over cobblestones. No more waiting for bags at
baggage claim. No more lost luggage. And no more anxiety.
I'm a liberated light traveler - and so will you be!

> "I travel light. I think the most important thing is to be in a good mood and enjoy life, wherever you are."
>
> DIANE VON FURSTENBERG

How to be a good light traveller: the Ten Commandments

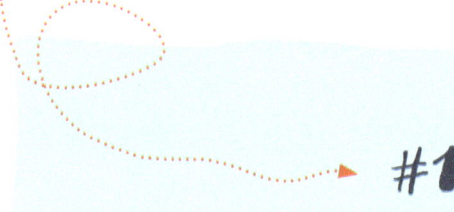

#1

Plan your trip

At the start of any travel adventure, it is important to plan your trip. The four essential considerations are:
Where will you be going? How long you will stay away?
What are the essential things you have to take with you?
What will you be doing while away?

Once you've answered these questions, it will be easy to pack accordingly.

#2

Create a packing list

Write or sketch a packing list. This is helpful to plan what you need to take with you, but also for what you can leave behind.

Think of three different facets or aspects to your packing: your clothing; your toiletries, and your hand or shoulder bag.

Remember, even if you're travelling with one small carry on bag only, most airlines permit you to take a small handbag as well - but all your luggage has to fit into the 7 kgs limit.

#3

Pack light in a small suitcase

There are many, many good reasons for travelling with one small carry on bag only.

One of the most valuable reasons for travelling with a carry on bag only is that you do not have to wait at a baggage carousel for your luggage to arrive. This saves you time and lessens anxiety, particularly when you are fatigued after a longhaul flight.

#4

Do not take 'nice to have' things

It might be tempting to throw in an item of clothing that you haven't worn before. A top has been languishing in your wardrobe and you image you will wear it on holiday. Resist that temptation. There are a few reasons why you haven't worn that item before: it doesn't fit you; it doesn't match your wardrobe; the colour doesn't suit you. None of these things is going to improve when on holiday or travelling for business. Leave that item of clothing behind.

#5

Remember to pack light toiletries

Toiletries and cosmetics are surprisingly heavy. Weigh and consider every tube and jar before you take it with you. Do you need a moisturiser and a separate sunscreen? Can you combine these as one lotion?

Remember to consult your packing list and don't be tempted to throw in yet another 'nice to have'.

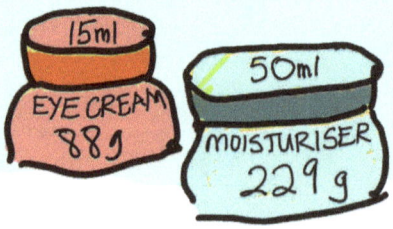

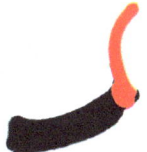

#6

Mix and match your wardrobe

Limit your wardrobe to one basic colour with a couple of different coloured tops for variety. Ensure that every piece of clothing works with all your other clothing. For example, can you wear your tops with your skirt, your shorts and your pants?

A constrained wardrobe makes choosing your clothes every morning easy. You spend less time managing, washing and packing clothes.

#7

Travel, walk and go out in the same shoes

Your shoes are your best friend. It's essential to fly, walk and travel in comfortable shoes. Find and choose shoes that can double up for more occasions. Just like your clothes, your shoes have to fit with your shorts, your skirt, your pants - and occasionally in the evening. No one notices your shoes when you travel, especially if they are an inconspicuous colour.

#8

Limit your holiday shopping

It's tempting to buy souvenirs and other mementos when you travel. But experiences always trump objects - so consider doing something that you'll remember for a long time and that has more meaning than another piece of clothing. Go paragliding, kayaking, hiking - whatever takes your fancy. And take home a digital photo as a souvenir.

#9

Carry your own bag

It is liberating carrying your own small bag over cobblestones, in and out of transport, up and down stairs and through airports. Knowing that you can lift your bag and run to catch a train, boat or plane is essential when travelling overseas, in foreign countries - or even in domestic airports.

#10

Thou shalt have fun!

The biggest bonus of travelling light is that you have fun!
No more wrangling with oversized suitcases.
No more concerns about lost luggage.
Less time spent getting ready in the mornings.

How to overcome your addiction to checked luggage

Learn to be a light traveler

I'M AN EXTREME LIGHT TRAVELER, BUT I DIDN'T HOP OUT OF THE LUGGAGE RACK FULLY ENLIGHTENED. IT'S TAKEN ME YEARS OF FLIGHTS, TRIPS AND TOURS TO MASTER THE ART OF LIGHT TRAVEL. THESE ARE SOME OF THE THINGS I LEARNED ALONG THE WAY, WHICH MIGHT HELP YOU OVERCOME *YOUR* ADDICTION TO CHECKED LUGGAGE.

Model your packing on yacht racing

A long time ago, I was persuaded by a boyfriend to go deep-sea yacht racing with him. For two years, I did this every second weekend.

Weight is an issue on a racing yacht, particularly a small one like ours was. I was only permitted one small bag, which I had to load and unload myself - sometimes jumping precariously from tender to yacht, carrying my bag and other supplies. I had to pull on my waterproofs, boots and all, in the low-ceilinged cabin, where we occasionally slept, prepared food and used the bucket (you know what for . . .) Talk about living and travelling in a tight space!

Planning and packing for yacht racing was excellent preparation for flying and travelling - and surviving - with few possessions. I'm not suggesting you take up yacht racing, but if you participate in a similar activity, like camping and hiking, you're most probably already prepared for light travel.

Yachting taught me not only how to pack lightly, but to manage with few clothes and fewer niceties - and I survived!

Holiday in a mobile home

Mobile homes are wonderful holiday vehicles: compact, comfortable, easy to drive, but small on packing space. My first trip around New Zealand was in a mobile home, which was a little like yachting, but less restrictive - you can stop to get out of the vehicle.

By the time of this trip, many years after the yachting experiences, I was already a lighter traveller, but Mr PetMan (aka Mr Graham) was still addicted to his large luggage.

Mr PetMan's large red suitcase led to conflict and discomfort - it's funny in hindsight - but he learnt through that experience: there's no need to pack *all* your possessions for every trip.

Think of your next trip like packing for a mobile home where every little thing has to have its place on board. This will help you to better consider how and what you *really need* next time you embark on a voyage.

Lighten your cosmetics load

For years my toiletries bag was like a graveyard for discarded toiletries - both opened and unopened. My approach was, 'Oh, I'll take that sample face mask/exfoliator/skin balm so that I can use it on holiday.' And guess what? I never used it. I didn't use those products at home - so why would I use them on holiday? The face mask/exfoliator/skin balm looks appealing, but it just takes up space.

These days I'm merciless in culling unnecessary products, packages and pills. I weigh all my toiletries: you'd be surprised how heavy cosmetics and toiletries can be.

Be ruthless when packing your cosmetics and toiletries: only take the essentials; leave the nice-to-haves at home. You'll be amazed and grateful how much lighter your luggage will be.

Pack for a weekend away

Do you fly long distance to visit friends or family? In Australia that's quite common. Next time you do, pack as if you're going for a weekend only. I promise you will survive with a carefully curated wardrobe, one (maybe two) pairs of shoes, and a small selection of cosmetics. You can always borrow or buy something that you may have left behind.

Planning and packing for a short break is good practice for managing overseas travel with one small bag. The thing that I find most liberating when staying with family is that my small suitcase fits easily into the spare bedroom - just like staying in a Tokyo hotel!

Stop shopping

If you've followed my advice, by now you'll have learnt how to prepare and pack for light travel. You've practised and succeeded in travelling with one small bag only. Your last hurdle is to stop shopping when you travel.

I remember when you *had* to go to Italy (those who could afford it) to buy the best sandals. Or you could only buy the latest fashions by visiting the boutiques of Britain.

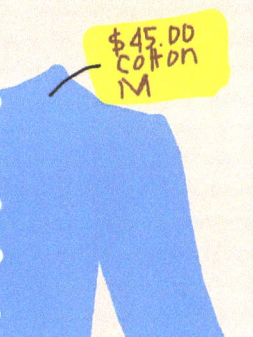

I even remember the days when you gave and brought back - well my family did - heaps of presents. These days, you can buy anything online - so why burden yourself with *things*. If you want a souvenir, snap a photo. Or enjoy an experience - it's so much more memorable.

De-tox travel

Well done: by this stage you've practised techniques to cut down on weight, clothes and unnecessary items. You've even travelled with only one small bag. How does that feel? Pretty good, I hope.

I don't mean to complain unnecessarily, but another major reason for travelling with carry on luggage only is that your bags will never get lost by the airlines. I've had my bags mislaid - *once for six weeks* - at least five times. That's reason enough *not* to check in your bags.

My advice: don't spend thirty travel years - like I did - before lightening your load. Wean yourself off that addiction of checked luggage today. Your hands, heart and travel soul will thank you for it.

What colour is your wardrobe?

When I look at photos of myself at 18, 28, 48 or even now, I still dress the same: sporty tailored is my fashion style. A long time ago I read that one should only ever wear two colours at the same time - and that formula works for me. The colours have adjusted a little over time: I may have started off with black + another colour; these days I wear grey + another colour as the grey complements my hair colour.

If you don't know what colour suits you, don't worry, that won't make planning your travel wardrobe more challenging: there's help at hand. Back in the 1980s, there was a trend to 'colour your style'. The thinking was that everyone's colouring is one of the following seasonal palettes: 'winter', 'summer', 'spring' or 'autumn'. Each 'season' comes with a colour selection that is ideally suited for your particularly 'colour style'. This seasonal palette is based on your hair, eye and skin colour - and believe me, it works.

Once you know what colours work for your particular 'season', packing for your trip becomes so much easier. You choose a foundation colour - mine as I said is either black or grey - to build your basic wardrobe. And then you add

touches of colour based on your seasonal palette. It is easy and practical, very much like my Planepack clothing list: simple, stylish and practical. If you prefer to travel with a wide range of frills and ruffles, Planepack might not be for you.

Time travel

When I visualize days and weeks, I see them as rods, each one representing a day of the week. The rods are all different colours while the weekend has the same for both days (Saturday is a little darker in tone). If that sounds strange, I'd be interested to know what your days and weeks look like. In my mind, days and weeks are neat and orderly, following the same structure. Mr PetMan has a different view of future time: his is nowhere near as structured as mine. I suspect his days are shrouded in mist . . .

Having this kind of view of the near future helps me to prepare for my trip: I visualize - fairly broadly - what I'll be doing on each of the days away. lay out my whole travel wardrobe on my bed before I pack. That way I can see what I'm taking with me as well as identifying what I've forgotten. I check that everything works with everything else.

For example, during a recent trip to Europe, I knew that I'd be in Belgrade for three days where I'd be visiting family, walking, exploring the city. Knowing that, I visualize the clothes and combinations that I need for that part of my stay. The latter part of my stay (13 days) was spent in Montenegro. I knew that I'd be going to the beach, but I'd also be walking, exploring ancient cities, going on a boat, dining out and strolling in sophisticated Porto Montenegro. So while I don't visualize each day's particular wardrobe, I know that I need a mixture of casual with slightly smarter clothes.

When I eventually pack for this kind of trip, I only take clothes that I will wear: I never take along any impulsive items that I think, 'Oh, it would be nice to wear that'. I'm restrained in picking my wardrobe: each piece of clothing has to work; nothing comes along for a free flight.

Weekend getaways

A good way to test your planning, packing and wardrobe skills is to trial the theory on a short trip: a weekend away might be the start of a new habit. I recently spent a few days in Melbourne, flying down on Friday evening and returning on Monday morning. I needed a mix of

warmer and summer clothes as the weather was a bit fresh. I packed day wear for gallery visits and smarter casual for evening dining. I left home with 6.8 kgs of luggage. Sadly when I came back I had to buy extra cabin luggage allowance - not that the extra weight was due to clothes, but to Christmas presents from the Melbourne family.

Bedecked with jewels - or not

'I hate packing,' sighed my friend Shelly. 'I take hours agonizing what jewellery to take with me.'

My advice is to take a favorite piece that you can wear for any occasion during your trip. Take jewellery that you are happy to wear every day. My standard jewellery is one pair of earrings, one ring (in addition to my wedding band), one necklace for everyday wear and one standout necklace for the evening. Believe me, it works! And once you've decided on your basic jewellery, you never again have to fuss about taking a whole lot of stuff that you're not going to wear. In addition, you're not going to worry about losing or having jewellery stolen during your travels as you'll be wearing your jewels all the time. Planepack is all about simplicity, style and ease of travel.

What's the
Planepack
essential
packing list?

WHAT DO YOU NEED TO PACK WITH YOU WHEN YOU TRAVEL? MY FRIENDS OFTEN ASK: 'WHAT DO I NEED TO CARRY WITH ME?' THIS IS MY ESSENTIAL WARDROBE WHICH IS ENOUGH TO KEEP YOU COMFORTABLE AND STYLISH FOR THREE WEEKS OR MORE.

When I talk about the colours and use the term neutral I refer to *your* preferred neutral colour. As I'm a winter - remember the colour style file? - my preferred neutral colour is black or grey. Yours may be a different colour depending on what your colour preferences are. What's important is to ensure that every item you pack works with every other item. All your tops should just as easily be worn with your skirt, your shorts or your pants. And your jacket and wrap should be interchangeable with any of your tops and match in style to your bottoms. I learnt a long time ago to wear a maximum of two colours. So my travel wardrobe is constrained. My two colours are usually black and grey. And I add a few brightly coloured tops to enhance these.

Planepack *packing list*

- Let's start off with some foundation garments. I take along two bras - one black and one tan or flesh coloured.

- I take five pairs of black knickers.

- I take two or three pairs of socks that match in colour to my comfortable shoes.

- I wear these shoes nearly every day so make sure they are just right. Wear them in before you travel.

- I take one pair of dressy sandals which might be flat or with a slight heel. And one pair of thongs for the beach.

- I take one pair of crease proof black, or another dark colour, pull-on lightweight slacks.

- I take one pair of shorts in a neutral colour preferably without pockets. I like shorts that are just above the knee, a bit like cycle shorts.

- I take one easy pull-on skirt in a neutral colour

- I like to add a bit of colour and pattern by taking along three - that's only three - t-shirts or smoothing tops or whatever you like to wear which can add that extra pop of colour to your neutral shades.

- I take one long sleeve wrap in a neutral colour.

- I take one pair of leggings in a neutral colour. I wear these on the plane.

- I take an unstructured jacket in a neutral colour which I wear on the plane.
- I take one crease proof evening top to go with my slacks.
- To dress up, I take what I call a 'killer' necklace - something that's got that va va voom look about it for the evenings. I don't usually wear this during the day. I do take an everyday necklace.
- I take one pair of earrings, which I don't wear on the plane because they make wearing my headphones - or sleeping - uncomfortable.
- I take one ring and my wedding ring.
- I take one silk scarf, which I wear on the plane. It's been suggested to me to buy a silk scarf next time I travel - rather than to take one from home.
- I take one bather.
- I take one beach sarong which I can dress up as a skirt if I need too. It's a very lightweight fabric so it dries easily.
- I take one thin strappy nightdress.
- I take one soft robe that rolls easily.

AND THAT'S IT! THAT'S MY TRAVEL WARDROBE FOR THREE WEEKS - AND BEST OF ALL, THE WEIGHT COMES IN AT ABOUT 5 KGS ONLY, LEAVING ENOUGH SPACE IN MY CARRY ON BAG FOR MY TOILETRIES.

Cosmetics and toiletries: what to pack?

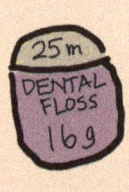

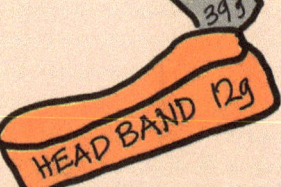

I recently published a podcast about
The Planepack Essential Travel List where I spoke
about the clothes I take with me for a two or
three week overseas trip. As mentioned, I travel and fly
with carry on luggage only. That means I carry on only
7 kgs in my hand luggage - and that has to accommodate
all my clothes plus my toiletries.

When I prepare and pack for an overseas trip, I usually
add my toiletries at the end. Cosmetics and toiletries,
as far as I'm concerned, are less important than clothes
and shoes: you can always buy small toiletry items as
you need them on holiday or when travelling. Packing
toiletries once I have all my clothes selected means
I can add or remove bottles and tubes to make sure
I'm under the permitted weight.

Size matters

When it comes to cosmetics, it is essential that you *carry on* products that are only 100 ml in size. That's 100 ml for toothpaste; 100 ml for shampoo, and so on. Airlines do *not* permit you to take liquids and lotions in bigger quantities. Don't make the mistake of taking any lotions that you've started to use where the quantity might be less than 100 ml, but is in a larger container. That 50 ml body lotion in the 200 ml bottle is going to be thrown away by the customs official; they don't have time to measure weight - they just go by what the number on the container states.

Similarly, don't forget that an impulse purchased bottle of wine will be dumped at customs - unless you buy duty-free bottles, which you are permitted to take on board. So leave those reds behind or buy duty-free if you must.

Talking about rules and regulations, I came across this recent update from the USA:

when it comes to liquids, the 3-1-1 rule still applies to carry-on bags. Liquids, gels, aerosols, creams and pastes must be 3.4 ounces [100 ml] or less per container; must be in 1-quart-sized [950 ml], clear, plastic, zip-top bag, and only one bag is allowed per passenger.

TSA: What not to carry on your flight, Tuesday, May 2nd 2017, 6:52 am AEST Tuesday, May 2nd 2017, 6:52 am AEST
By: Susanna Black, Weekend Anchor/Reporter

Based on their advice, your *total* amount of carry on cosmetics should not exceed 950 ml of content. Using this as a guide, my Planepack cosmetics list contains about 800 ml of content - well within the limit!

Planepack *cosmetics list*

This is my essential toiletries and cosmetics packing list:

- Toothbrush. I like an electric toothbrush. A charged electric toothbrush will have power to last for two weeks. It's your decision to take the charger, or after two weeks' battery powers, switch to use the electric toothbrush as a traditional toothbrush.
- Toothpaste
- Moisturiser
- Cleanser
- Cotton cleanser pads
- Earbuds
- Body lotion (if not staying at hotels)
- Shampoo (if not staying at hotels)
- Conditioner (if not staying at hotels) - Hotels usually supply sample bottles of shampoo, conditioner and body lotion.
- Sun tan lotion: I buy sun tan lotion at my destination.

- Perfume (one thing I cannot do without; I usually take a new 50 ml bottle with me as a summer treat.)

- Makeup. I only use lipstick. It's up to you to take whatever makeup you think is absolutely necessary.

- Medications. I take an antiseptic gel and headache pills. Mr PetMan takes tummy sickness prevention pills. I empty medications from their boxes and take only the blister packs: less packaging means less weight.

- Samples: I collect cosmetics samples during the year and take these. They are light and easy to pack and carry, and I find it fun to try out new products when I'm on holiday.

A few final tips

My advice is: don't stress too much about toiletries and cosmetics - unless you're travelling in remote areas where you absolutely cannot buy any. Take just the essentials - and have fun trying out new brands while you're on holiday.

One word of caution though, if you're buying lotions and shampoos overseas, you might find it challenging to get these in small amounts or travel-size packs. In Australia it's easy to buy small containers; I didn't find it that easy in Europe. I solved this by swapping or giving away any unused lotions to a friend or family member. You can decant what you need into your small containers - and give the rest away. If you don't have small containers, pharmacies usually have these for purchase - or they give them away with certain products.

Next time you travel, lay out your cosmetics and toiletries like you would your clothes - and consider what you absolutely need - and what you can do without. You might be surprised how much lighter your carry on luggage will be.

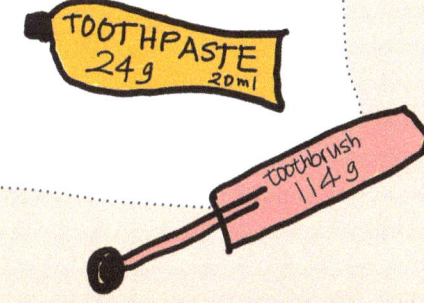

My luggage, my father and his ashes (lost luggage story #1)

My father was born and lived in Serbia - the former Yugoslavia. After World War 2, he escaped the Communist regime and in December 1955 he, my mother and my sister disembarked ship at Cape Town harbour. I was born the following April in Johannesburg and raised in Cape Town.

My parents adored Serbia but sadly my father never returned, fearing retribution for his escape. When he died in 1990, my father's body was cremated and we interred the ashes at Maitland Cemetery. Eight years later, when we decided to migrate to Australia, I couldn't bear the thought of leaving my father's ashes behind. I had the urn exhumed and we brought his ashes to Wagga Wagga, packed inside my school suitcase.

For a long time, I intended to sprinkle my father's ashes in his beloved Belgrade, but it was another 10 years before my mother and I journeyed to the old country and I had the opportunity to take my father's ashes with me. I had an inkling that I might need permission to travel with human remains, but I ignored that thought.

Packing the ashes

On the morning of our trip, Mr PetMan unearthed the ashes from the suitcase - now in our garage.

'These ashes are so heavy,' I said with dismay. 'I had no idea human remains weigh so much.'

I decided to take some of the ashes only.

'My father won't know the difference,' I assured Mr PetMan as I ladled ashes into a Tupperware container, jamming it into my suitcase.

My mother and I flew to Europe through Dubai. The trip went well - notwithstanding my mother's excess baggage and overweight suitcase - and we arrived in Belgrade early the next morning. In the arrivals hall, I dragged my mother's bag off the conveyor belt and waited for mine. I guess you know the outcome: my bag never arrived. Our argument with the Serbian airport authorities didn't produce my suitcase. We caught a taxi to my aunt's flat, my mother swearing in the back seat.

Losing the ashes

I spent three weeks in Europe, but my bag was elsewhere. Each day my mother encouraged me to shout over the phone at the JAT employees and airport officials - but still my bag remained lost. I was mortified: what if the Dubai officials had impounded my suitcase when they spotted a powder they mistook for cocaine? What if they imprisoned me? I was returning alone; who would rescue me if I languished in a Dubai jail? Added to my anxiety was the thought that my father's ashes were trundling around a baggage carousel - lost forever because of me.

At the end of my holiday, I flew back to Australia through Dubai - without any arrest or questions - arriving safely in Canberra.

Regaining the ashes

Three weeks later my mother phoned me from Belgrade:

'Your bag haf arrived,' she said, indignant at the errant suitcase. 'Vot you vant me to do wit it?'

'Send it back to Australia,' I responded, 'but take out Daddy's ashes so you can sprinkle them in Belgrade.

Are they still in the bag?'

'Vel there's some sandy in your clothes. But I take it out,' she replied.

I imagined my mother and my aunt muttering: 'She haf no respect for poor Branko and his ashes.'

Sprinkling the ashes

As it turned out, my mother didn't sprinkle my father's ashes - she said it rained too much during her stay.

For four years my father's ashes remained in the Tupperware container before my aunt sprinkled them from a Belgrade bridge - on the day of my mother's funeral. Finally my father - or at least some part of him - was home. We still have his ashes in the garage - but that's another story . . .

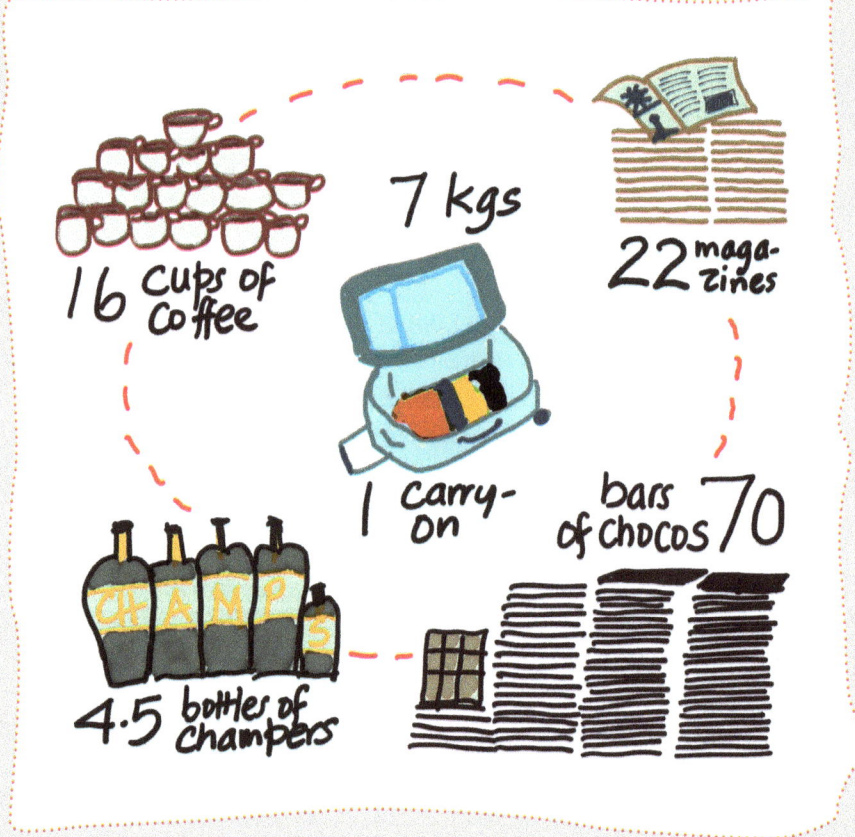

Why carry on travel is easier

- Life is easier with one bag only: less chance of losing one bag or having it stolen.
- You won't have to wait in line to check in your bags.
- It's easier to travel and carry your bag into boats, trains, planes and buses.
- Packing and unpacking are so easy: fewer clothes make for a simpler life. Minimalism reduces stress.
- Lighter bags are much easier to carry
- There's less chance the airline might lose your bag.
- Best of all, you no longer have to wait at the baggage carousel for a bag that might never appear: stride out of customs like a rock star!

What do other readers say about Planepack?

I'm still learning about packing lightly! Thanks for the hints — **CHRISTINA**

Thank you Slobodanka, great article and handy for me as I'll be travelling to Rome from Melbourne in October. I'll then be spending a few weeks travelling through Italy, Slovenia and Hungary. I want my luggage to be as light as possible so I don't have to rely on my husband to haul it on and off buses and trains for me. Each time I travel I always vow to take less next time so this has given me lots of ideas xx — **ANNE**

Lots of good tips. I was forced to cram everything from my Large suitcase into my Med. sized one on my last trip. It was STUFFED to the Brim, but didn't exceed the WEIGHT limit. I hope THAT hasn't changed in the last 2 yrs. — SHARON

Thank you for this article which is extremely timely as I will be heading off on a 5 week tour of Australia with my sister in October/November and do not want to load myself down with unnecessary luggage. I shall certainly use your guidelines when putting together my final packing list. — JANET

Useful tips — IRENKE

Great article! I read Color Me Beautiful *35 years ago and knowing what it taught me has made life much simpler!!* — ANITA

EXPER-IENCES

Want to travel and fly the Planepack way?

For expert tips and advice for women (and men!) who want to travel light.

Check into the Planepack website at
www.planepack.com.au

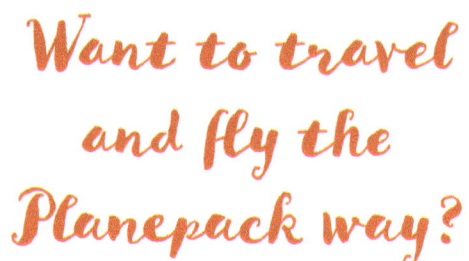

www.ingramcontent.com/pod-product-compliance
Lightning Source LLC
Chambersburg PA
CBHW061119010526
44112CB00024B/2920